CW01513308

# The Funny to Running

### Excuses, Obsessions, and the Hilarious Truth about Runners

**Ricky Woods**

Copyright © 2025 Ricky Woods

Published by: Bemberton Ltd

All rights reserved. No part of this book or any portion thereof may be reproduced in any form by any electronic or mechanical means, without permission in writing from the publisher, except for the use of brief quotes in a book review.

The publisher accepts no legal responsibility for any action taken by the reader, including but not limited to financial losses or damages, both directly or indirectly incurred as a result of the content in this book.

ISBN: 978-1-918027-00-6

Disclaimer: The information in this book is general and designed to be for information only. While every effort has been made to ensure it is wholly accurate and complete, it is for general information only. It is not intended, nor should it be taken as professional advice. The author gives no warranties or undertakings whatsoever concerning the content.

View all our books at **bemberton.com**

# CONTENTS

# INTRODUCTION:
# WELCOME TO THE CULT

**Congratulations — you're a runner.**

Or maybe you aren't.

You might've landed on these pages because you've befriended a runner... or, even worse, married one.

No matter. Whether you lace up your shoes day after day to inflict unnecessary harm on yourself, or you simply watch a loved one do the same thing, this book is for you. It's a peek behind the curtain at the ridiculous world of running — all the things everyone sees but no one dares to say out loud.

# THIS IS *NOT* A TRAINING GUIDE

The last thing the world needs is another running guide.

Oh, it's a good idea to start slow and build up to a 5K? You don't say! Tell me more!

Please. Enough already. Let's stop pretending training for a race is rocket science. You just run for a while one day, then do it again the next. If you stack enough of those days together, you'll probably make it to race day. More likely, you'll quit after a week or get injured long before then. But, of course, the training guides never mention *that* part.

Rest assured, this is not a training manual. Not even close. You won't need your heart-rate monitor. And whatever you do, please don't apply anti-chafing cream while reading. That's a mental image no one needs.

If you're here for coaching tips, you're in the wrong place. You'd be better off having another long, emotional conversation with your foam roller while rocking in pain.

## WARNING SIGNS YOU'VE JOINED THE CULT

This early in the book, you might still be in denial.

You may not think you're a "real" runner. Or you may not believe your loved one has fully fallen into the trap.

But by the end of this book, the truth will be unavoidable.

For now, let's ease you in — a warm-up lap, if you will — with a few early warning signs that you're already deep in the cult.

- Your browser history includes things like "best anti-chafe cream," "tempo vs threshold run," and "how long do toenails take to grow back."

- You know what a "tempo run" is... and explain it to strangers who didn't ask.

- You spent more time choosing your last pair of shoes than your last car.

- Your idea of a relaxing Sunday is a 6 a.m. alarm and a 10-mile run at race pace.

- You can say "fartlek" without giggling.

- You own two wine glasses... and ten water bottles.

- Your laundry smells like sweat and regret.

- You've planned at least one "racecation."

- A broken phone is fine. A malfunctioning GPS watch is a full-scale tragedy.

- You firmly believe: *If it's not on Strava, it didn't happen.*

Yeah. I thought so. You've joined the cult.

## THE SLIPPERY SLOPE
## (A.K.A. THE EVOLUTION OF A RUNNER)

You didn't mean to get this deep.

Maybe you just wanted to get fitter. Maybe you lost a bet. Maybe you downloaded Couch to 5K and thought, *"How bad can it be?"*

But that's how it starts. Innocent jogs turn into training plans. One pair of shoes becomes six. You start talking about "fueling," signing up for races you don't remember registering for, and nodding along to conversations about cadence like you're not completely lost.

This book will guide you through the stages — from the wide-eyed Optimist to the fully broken-in, Strava-addicted Lifer.

It's a journey all runners take (whether they admit it or not). You'll see yourself somewhere on the path. And once you do... well, there's no un-seeing it.

## IT'S TOO LATE TO TURN BACK NOW

Not only is it too late to back out of this book — it's too late to escape the lifestyle. You're in now. There's no going back to normal life. Not that you'd want to, anyway.

Once those first few miles were logged, the runner's descent began. Your fate was sealed. It's out of your hands now.

Sure, you could've taken up knitting. Or piano. Or woodworking. But no. You chose running — and with it, a future of black toenails, foam rolling, and GPS-induced anxiety.

We'd love to tell you it's all going to be fine. But we honestly don't know that's true.

So, lace 'em up tight. It's going to be a wild ride, but we hope you enjoy the journey. And read fast — you've got a training schedule to keep up with, after all.

# PHASE 1

# THE OPTIMIST (BRIGHT-EYED, BLISTER-FREE, AND DOOMED)

# THE ARC OF A RUNNER (NOVICE TO LYCRA-CLAD MANIAC)

**1**

No one starts out intending to become a "runner." Sure, you might decide to go for a few runs — maybe to get in shape, lose a bit of weight, or prove something to yourself (or your smug coworker). But that doesn't mean you expected to become a runner in every sense of the word.

And yet, that's exactly what happens to all of us. One day you're casually signing up for a local 5K to support a good cause. The next, you're standing in a chemist trying to discreetly ask where they keep the anti-chafing cream — because your nipples got shredded on a 15-mile training run. What the hell went wrong?

Every runner goes through a version of this. You might think you're the exception. You're not. This is the path. And it's beautiful. And absurd.

Take comfort in this: you're not alone. Not even close. Countless others have descended the same slippery slope — stage by stage — until their friends and family no longer recognise them. (Nor do they recognise themselves, to be fair.

Don't think that will happen to you? It's probably already started. You just haven't noticed. So let's walk through the four stages of the runner life cycle — and figure out where you are on the spectrum. It'll all make sense soon. Sort of.

# STAGE ONE: THE OPTIMIST

Everything is sunshine and roses at the start. Even when the runs are hard, they're still weirdly rewarding. With each mile that passes, you feel more confident in your new hobby. Your split times are starting to fall. The endorphins are real. There's no telling what the future could hold.

Okay — so you recently had to Google "How long is a 10K?", and you still mostly pick your running shoes based on how pretty they are. But that doesn't mean you're destined to remain a novice forever.

One of the fascinating parts of this stage is that you still feel hesitant to talk about your runs with other people. You're proud of what you're doing, but not confident enough to bring it up in conversation — and definitely not ready to compare yourself to *actual* runners.

So far, the joy you get from running is internal. You've lost a little weight. Going up the stairs at your office is easier than it's been in years. When someone brings up running in conversation, you deflect the topic and maybe say something like "Yeah, I go for a run every once in a while." You don't yet own the title of "runner." But that day is coming.

You may even enter your first race during this optimistic, naive phase. It's probably just a 5K, but it's exciting. So exciting, in fact, that when they hand you a free t-shirt, you immediately put it on. Rookie move — but totally on brand for Stage One.

Nothing can dampen your enthusiasm at this point. Not even the looming spectre of injuries. Despite the fact that almost all runners eventually get injured, you push this reality out of your mind and assume it won't happen to you. After all, your legs feel great — what could possibly go wrong?

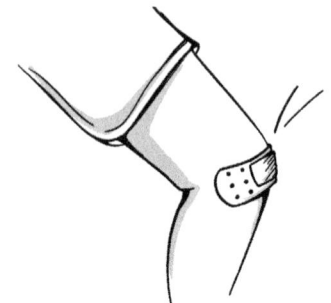

If you only knew what lay ahead.

## STAGE TWO: THE OBSESSOR

There won't be a single moment — or even a single day — when you cross over from naïve optimist to full-blown obsessive. It happens slowly and subtly, until one day you look up and realise there are six pairs of running shoes by your front door... despite having just one pair of feet.

Speaking of shoes, an obsession with gear is a hallmark of this stage. Where you once threw on an old t-shirt and whatever shorts were clean, you now spend hours researching "ideal performance fabrics."

You start saying the phrase *moisture-wicking* in casual conversation. A review of your credit card statement suggests you are training for the Olympics, even though you are just jogging a few miles three times a week in your neighborhood.

A few months ago, you didn't even know what a hydration vest was. Now, you can't imagine leaving the house without one.

The gear purchases might be superfluous and expensive, but by far the worst part of this stage of the running lifecycle is the conversation. My God, the conversation.

Running is all you talk about. Every chat, whether personal or professional, is another opportunity to "impress" others with your efforts. You transition right into running talk so quickly and naturally that you forget to notice one key factor — NO ONE ASKED!!!

Now, to be clear: talking about running *with other runners* is fine. It's a shared obsession. A bonding tool. A healthy outlet. Talking about your hobby when the other person doesn't give a sh*t is a great way to burn bridges and not get invited back to a dinner party.

At this stage, running has taken over and there is no turning back. You now use your foam roller more than your sofa — or your toothbrush. Sitting in front of the TV in the evening usually involves a massage gun, and you refer to food now as 'fuel'. Sure, you might be obsessed, but this combination of steely focus and expensive gear is going to lead to great things.

You've never felt more in-tune with your body. You are obsessed with data. Heart rate tracking is a non-negotiable part of your day, whether you are running or not. A decline in your resting heart rate is an emotional victory worthy of its own Strava post.

Not long ago, running 10 miles was a once-a-year feat. Now it's just another Sunday morning.

You've come a long way, and there is still so much to look forward to. Running has become your life and you wouldn't trade it for the world.

## STAGE THREE: THE PHILOSOPHER

Somehow, that vision of yourself cruising to a win and earning the respect of your fellow runners never quite came to life. There were a few PRs along the way, but the injuries piled up, and your progression suddenly slowed.

Your body has started to betray you.

A few years ago, you bounced back from a long run with nothing more than a shower and a smug Instagram post. Now, you finish and immediately reach for ice packs, compression sleeves, and a tub of anti-inflammatory cream the size of a paint can.

You've spent more time Googling your symptoms than actually training. Is it tendonitis? A stress reaction? Just "tight hips"? No one knows. Not even your physio — and you've seen three.

Somewhere along the way, your mindset changed. You used to train for goals. Now you train *around* injuries. The running hasn't stopped, but it's definitely slowed — and not just your pace.

No matter what race you enter, someone just a little fitter, a little faster, and a little younger always seems to show up next to you on the start line.

But that's okay. This is still a great hobby... right? You still love the sport just as much as the day you started.

Right?

As your experience grows, you tell yourself running is about more than times. It's about the *experience*. All those hours logged on trails and tracks have taught you life lessons. You're grounded now. Patient. Wise. Running is a moving meditation — and you, naturally, are a sage.

At least, that's the persona you've adopted. Inside, you're still quietly furious. Why can't you hit those times anymore? How are these other runners so damn fast? They can't possibly be clean. You're convinced that everyone ahead of you is doping — even if this is just a charity 10K with a banana at the finish.

And as much as you go on and on about "the journey," let's be honest — the only person you're trying to convince is yourself. Despite the frustration and low-grade existential disappointment with your running "career," you keep showing up. You keep logging miles.

At least, until a better hobby comes along.

## STAGE FOUR: THE LIFER

A better hobby never came along. You are now a lifer.

You'll never win a race, and your PBs are probably behind you, but unlike before, you've truly accepted that fact. It doesn't matter.

At this point, you're not even sure why you run. You just do. Like breathing. Like sleeping. Like paying bills. Running is part of your identity now — involuntary, unquestioned, automatic. Your friends and family — much like most of your toenails — have given up long ago.

No one in your life can understand the stubborn determination behind your daily run. Absolutely nothing will stop you. You don't even think about skipping a run. Bad weather? Whatever. Sore knees? Please — there hasn't been cartilage in those joints for years.

You still run every day, but you've long since stopped keeping track. Your GPS watch is dead, lost, or outdated. You don't care. You measure runs by feel now. By landmarks. By how long it takes you to get from one porta-loo to the next.

Performance is gone. Pretence is gone. What's left is peace. Durable shoes. And a strong sense of direction — mostly bathroom-related.

## POP QUIZ: WHICH PHASE ARE YOU IN?

Still not sure where you land on the runner life cycle? We've put together a quick quiz to help you narrow down your location.

Answer these five questions, total your score, and find out just how far gone you really are.

- Each (a) answer = 1 point

- (b) = 2 points

- (c) = 3 points

- (d) = 4 points

1. How many pairs of running shoes do you own?
   a. One — They were the cheapest ones I could find at the store.
   b. Two or three — I rotate them based on terrain and weather conditions.
   c. Four or more — I can recite the specs of each pair from memory.
   d. No idea — There are more running shoes in my house than blisters on my feet.

2. When someone asks about your weekend, you say:
   a. "Good — did some yard work and went for a jog."
   b. "Great — logged a 10-miler and a recovery run."
   c. "Amazing — I shaved 13 seconds off my mile pace. Want to see the Strava data?"
   d. "Brutal. I had to spend the whole time with the family and didn't run at all."

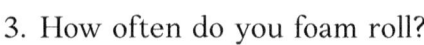

3. How often do you foam roll?
   a. What's a foam roller?
   b. Only when something hurts.
   c. I do a few minutes of rolling in the morning to get things loosened up.
   d. I sleep on a bed of foam rollers so my muscles stay activated all night.

4. What is your response when you fail to set a PR?
   a. "No big deal — I'll get it next time."

b. "Disappointing... but I still enjoyed the run."

c. "Won't get over it for a week. Avoid me."

d. "Stopped by the running store to yell at the salesperson who sold me these sh*tty shoes."

5. How long has it been since you purchased running gear (not shoes)?

a. I didn't know runners needed anything other than shoes.

b. I picked up a couple of shirts and some shorts at a clearance sale.

c. My monthly credit card statement has a category labeled "Running Addiction."

d. I have five subscriptions that deliver new gear to my doorstep every Friday.

How did you fare?

If your score is under 10, congratulations — you may just have a healthy relationship with this crazy sport. For those of you in the 10–15 range, there may still be time to prevent this from getting out of hand. If you are above 15 — or, God forbid, all the way at 20 — your fate is sealed. Welcome to the cult. Lycra, foam rollers, and denial await.

You'll see echoes of these stages throughout the chapters ahead. That's because runners — no matter how different they seem — follow eerily similar patterns. And as tragic as that might be, it's also hilarious (when viewed from a safe distance).

Maybe you're just starting out in **Stage One**, still pretending the later stages won't apply to you. Or maybe you're deep into **Stage Four**, chuckling at the bright-eyed newbies who still think they'll "just do one race."

Wherever you are on the spectrum — we're glad you're here. Now ice your knees, suck on your energy gel, and enjoy the book.

# RUNNING GEAR YOU TOTALLY NEED (BUT DEFINITELY DON'T)

**2**

One of the appealing things about running is how little equipment you *actually* need to get started. A pair of shoes, a t-shirt, and some shorts — done. Hell, if you've got enough confidence, you might not even need the shirt.

Given the fundamental simplicity of running, you might think it would be hard for businesses to make a fortune off a sport that, in theory, requires almost nothing. Oh, how wrong you'd be. Running is big business — bafflingly so from the outside. Do these people just enjoy giving away their money?

Somehow, running has become a full-blown gear sport. That label used to be reserved for activities like cycling, where the need for equipment is at least somewhat obvious. In running? Not obvious at all. And yet here we are — with entire empires built on selling overpriced "essentials" to sweaty optimists.

This chapter takes a closer look at the absurdity of modern running gear. By the time we're done, you'll think twice before pulling out your credit card for another $300 impulse purchase.

Make no mistake — you'll *still* buy it. But at least you'll hesitate first.

# THE SHOE SPIRAL

We start with the most reasonable of all running gear purchases: the shoes. On the surface, this category actually makes sense. Sure, there are a few maniacs out there pounding pavement in bare feet, but that fad  has (mostly) come and gone — though physios are still raking it in from the damage it left behind. For the most part, runners wear shoes. For obvious reasons.

So, we won't give you too much grief for wanting a pair of running shoes.

Note the phrasing: **a pair**. Not five. Not ten.

Some runners stack so many shoes by the front door they spend more time choosing a pair than running the first mile.

Of course, it starts innocently enough — just one pair. Or maybe two, if you dabble in both roads and trails. That's reasonable, right? You tell yourself that's all you'll ever need.

Until you read that Max Cushioning shoes are great for lighter recovery days. And then you discover that Race Shoes are lighter and will shave seconds off your time. And don't forget that you'll need backups for all of these different pairs, so you can rotate and "keep them fresh".

And then there's the carbon plate spiral.

Once reserved for Olympic legends like Eliud Kipchoge — you know, the guy who ran a marathon in under two hours — carbon-plated "super shoes" are now seen on every suburban tarmac from New York to Napa.

The difference? Kipchoge was fast. And paid to wear them.

You are... neither.

Even that mountain of shoes might be forgivable if not for the prices. **My God, the prices.**

When did a basic pair of running shoes start costing $150? And if you, for some reason, decide you "need" elite racing super shoes, you're looking at prices north of $300. For sneakers. That you will actively sweat in.

At least they'll last you for years at that price, right? Yeah, not so much. For some reason, the more you spend, the faster they seem to fall apart.

You may only get 100 miles out of a high-end pair before you have to pull out your credit card again.

Here's a tip: **If you aren't being paid to wear elite running shoes, you're not an elite runner.**

You are just another sucker — ahem — customer. So if you find yourself *not* wearing your nicest pair because you're afraid to get them dirty, those weren't running shoes. They were a financial mistake.

## SOCKS & COMPRESSION MADNESS

Surely we can find some sanity in the sock department, right? There's no way runners have fallen for a marketing scheme that convinces them they need *magic socks* just to go for a jog... right? They're socks. You can get three pairs for $10.

Nope. Not even socks are safe.

Even here — and in their distant cousin, compression sleeves — runners have taken the bait hook, line, and fully-supported calf.

Let's start with the basics. Did you know there are running socks labeled *right* and *left*? Of course you did. There's a $20 pair on your feet right now — made from quick-drying, anti-blister, arch-supporting, nano-engineered yarn harvested from clouds or whatever.

And just when you think it can't get dumber, in come **toe socks** — also known as gloves for your feet. Because nothing says "peak performance" like struggling to fit your pinky toe into its own dedicated compression tube. They promise better grip, fewer blisters, and "natural toe splay." They also promise that you'll still be single by the end of your run.

Naturally, all these socks are marketed as high-tech essentials. Quick-drying. Compression-enhanced. Precision-cushioned. Moisture-evaporating. All yours for the price of a steak dinner.

Will they make you go further? Maybe. Will they make you faster? Doubtful. Will they make you look like you know what you're doing? Also doubtful — especially if you've paired them with neon calf sleeves and a hydration belt the size of a toddler's life vest.

Speaking of those calf sleeves: what exactly are we compressing here? Hopes? Regret?

If you think wrapping tight synthetic fabric around your legs is going to magically ward off shin splints, you've got another thing coming. The only thing those sleeves are successfully compressing is your **wallet**.

But hey — at least you look like you know what you're doing. And in running, that's half the battle.

# YOUR GPS OVERLORD

Everywhere you run, you are being watched. No, not by a secret admirer who thinks you look fantastic in those $100 shorts, but by your very own **GPS overlord** — dutifully strapped to your wrist, judging your every move.

You head out the door and instantly become a data stream. Every step, every turn, every poorly judged hill climb is tracked down to the inch. Doesn't sound very relaxing, does it?

RUN PRO

But hey, at least all that personal data is *private*, right? It's not like anyone else can see where you've been, how far you went, or how badly you bonked on mile four. Right?

Wait, what's that? What's *Strava*?

Oh boy. You're telling me you upload your workouts to a public platform for the world to see? That sounds like a terrible idea, if we're being honest. What's the point?

Strava *says* it's about encouragement, community, and sharing the joy of movement. In reality? It's about quiet comparison, passive-aggressive kudos, and proving you suffered more than Dave from work.

So you're locked in a childish, pointless battle with your friends and neighbors to see who can suffer the most, run the longest, or get the most kudos.

The modern runner mindset: "If it's not on Strava, it didn't happen." It's not about the sweat, the progress, or even the process. It's about the clout.

And the idea of running without your GPS master strapped to your wrist? Inconceivable. You've probably even skipped a run or two because your watch wasn't charged and couldn't record your every stride. A run without cadence data or blood-oxygen stats (or whatever else it tracks)? What would even be the point?

And to enjoy this level of data obsession, you'll need — yep, you guessed it — a watch the size of a train station clock strapped to your wrist. You know the ones. Usually accompanied by a smug look that says, *"Yes, I'm an athlete."*

Ask the wearer what time it is and they'll reply, "Would you like my altitude, barometric pressure, or VO$_2$ max while I'm at it?"

These monstrosities don't come cheap either. A Garmin — as you already know, because there's probably one on your wrist and another buried in your bedside drawer — will set you back $300 or more. But hey, you can't put a price on knowing your stride length in real-time. Apparently.

# ADDING BELTS & VESTS TO THE MIX

At some point, the running companies maxed out the market on ridiculously expensive shirts, shorts, and shoes. So that was it, right? They'd squeezed every dollar they could out of apparel?

Not even close.

With clothing tapped out, they turned their attention to a new "essential" category: belts and vests.

You know — the items you need to buy in order to carry all the *other* things you bought. It's a gear spiral within a gear spiral.

Now look, we get it. If you're heading out for a 50-mile ultra in the mountains, a hydration vest makes sense. You need a way to carry water, calories, maybe a GPS beacon in case you're mauled by a bear. That's reasonable.

But you're not in the mountains, are you? You're jogging a loop around your suburban neighborhood. Do you really need snacks and a litre of water when you'll be home in 45 minutes?

If you get that thirsty, just cut the run short and raid your own kitchen. The fridge is probably still within your GPS signal range anyway.

# BECOMING AN URBAN SOLDIER

When enough people in a community
pick up running, something strange
starts to happen: they begin competing
to look the most like a runner. Not *be*
the best runner — just *look* like one.
And that's when the gear war begins.

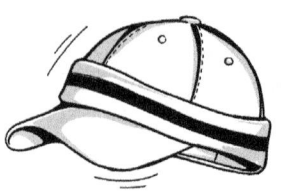

It starts innocently enough. A new shirt here, a fancy pair of
shoes there. But it escalates quickly. One piece of kit at a time,
until suddenly you're stepping out the front door looking like
a fully geared-up "Urban Soldier."

You're now wearing over $1,000 worth of tech, foam, mesh,
and Lycra — shoes with carbon plates, a watch that can survive
the Mariana Trench, compression sleeves for every limb, and
a hydration vest heavy enough to qualify as resistance training.

There's no doubt you're ready for battle. Only... there is no
battle. You're jogging a gentle 5K before heading home for
a warm shower and some admin emails.

It's a silly game of adult dress-up. But hey — if war *does* break
out between miles two and three, at least you'll be able to run
away really, really fast.

# MASTERING THE ART OF GEAR JUSTIFICATION

Runners aren't stupid. Gullible? Sure. But not stupid. Deep down, you know you don't *really* need all this gear. So, the only logical next step is to start justifying your purchases — not to others (okay, maybe your spouse), but to yourself.

Let's be honest: no one is asking about your gear. These justifications are entirely inward-facing — little pep talks to ease the sting of your dwindling bank balance.

Here are a few of the greatest hits. See how many you recognize:

- "I need the best gear to avoid injuries (even though I keep getting hurt)."

- "Each different type of run demands a different type of shoe."

- "Everyone in my running group has these shorts (and I'm a sheep)."

- "I didn't need another pair of shoes, but they were on sale."

- "Sure, they were $300, but they'll knock a second off my mile time."

- "Running gear is still cheaper than therapy."

Do you need fancy gear to be a mediocre weekend runner? Of course not — but since when has that stopped you or anyone else? Running gear is here to stay, and given how much you have spent on it over the last few years, that's probably a good thing.

# THE CAST OF RUNNER CHARACTERS YOU'LL MEET

## 3

Running is a great way to meet people. Some of those people will be more enjoyable to meet than others, of course, but you are sure to make a lot of new connections either way.

Sometimes it happens organically — two strangers passing on the path, one deep in their playlist, the other hellbent on starting a conversation anyway (because runners *will* talk, even to people clearly trying to avoid them).

When you start entering races, you'll quickly discover they're more than just a test of fitness — they're social hubs for the slightly unhinged. As your network of running acquaintances grows, a pattern begins to emerge: almost every runner fits

neatly into one of a few classic categories.

Below, we break down the most common characters you're bound to encounter. See how many sound familiar. (And yes, it's okay if one of them is you.)

# THE STRAVA ADDICT — "IF IT'S NOT ON STRAVA, IT DIDN'T HAPPEN"

In the previous chapter, we talked about the prominent role Strava plays in the life of today's runner. Most runners fall into the Strava rabbit hole at some point — but some fall harder than others. For a select few, Strava becomes their entire running personality, and the results are devastating (okay, maybe not devastating, but definitely embarrassing).

This runner doesn't just post all his runs on Strava — he uploads them *within moments* of finishing, complete with a dramatic, poetic title. When he's not running (or posting about running), he's scrolling Strava endlessly, hunting for more local.

Ah, the segments. It's not enough for this guy to race a few times a year — he needs to compete *every single day*. So he scours the map, finds Strava segments nearby, and sets off with domination in mind. One by one, he lays claim to these precious digital crowns... and returns immediately once someone dares to take one away.

RUN PRO

The number of Strava segments he owns is a direct reflection of his self-worth. And let's just say — he checks it often.

# THE GEARHEAD — "FULLY EQUIPPED, MARGINALLY FIT"

For some runners, gear serves as a stand-in for actual fitness. Sure, this runner hasn't hit a PR in years, but they *look* great out on the road. Their kit leans more toward aesthetics than performance — not that they'd ever admit it.

They'll insist every choice — from shoes to socks to gels and chews — is all about shaving those last few seconds off their time. None of it seems to be paying off, but that doesn't matter. Any day now, this investment is going to *click*, and they'll start striding away from the pack.

Spending all their money on gear is one thing — that's their problem. The bigger issue is they *also* want to fix *your* gear. They'll point out how the drop height of your shoes doesn't match your stride. Or how your shorts should be one inch shorter to reduce aerodynamic drag. Or some other nonsense.

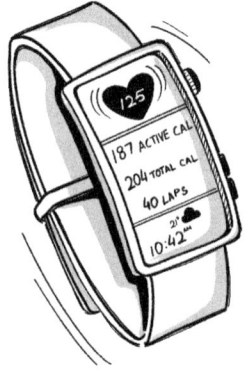

If we didn't know better, we'd say the Gearhead is just projecting their insecurities onto you by critiquing every item you own. But that couldn't be it... right?

# THE ZEN RUNNER — "IT'S ABOUT THE JOURNEY (BUT ALSO THE PRS)

There is something aspirational about encountering a Zen Runner. The name pretty much says it all here — this is a person that isn't obsessed with splits, or getting onto the podium. They simply want to enjoy the experience. We could all learn a lesson from such an attitude.

Unfortunately, there's just one problem with that attitude — it's a lie. If the Zen Runner was truly in touch with his inner self, he wouldn't go all out to sprint the last 200m to beat a few more people at the end of the local 5k. He also wouldn't elbow past you at the water station to get in and out as fast as possible. The message of the Zen Runner is one of peace and community — but his actions tell a very different story.

Somewhere out there, you could probably find a runner who is truly at peace. They genuinely don't care about where they finish and couldn't even tell you their PR for various distances. But that runner is hard to find — and, in the age of Strava and the data revolution, they are becoming even rarer. Speaking of the data revolution, our next runner is deep in spreadsheets and won't be climbing out of the hole anytime soon.

# THE DATA NERD— "TRAINING BY ALGORITHM"

More people than ever before make their living in front of a computer. These white-collar workers crunch numbers, run algorithms, write code, and generally do nerdy things. Those things are extremely useful for the world, and lucrative for their careers—but they're nerdy nonetheless.

So, what happens when such an individual picks up running as a hobby? They bring their data obsession with them. This runner isn't tuned into his body so much as he is tuned into the analytics. Whatever the numbers say to do, he will do—regardless of how it feels at the time.

This is the runner who's staring down at his watch, not just at mile splits, but at every possible moment. God forbid the Data Nerd heads into the woods for a trail run, because they're likely to wind up smacking into a pine tree while glassy-eyed, trying to absorb as much information as possible.

It only takes a moment of chatting with a Data Nerd to realize exactly what kind of runner you've encountered. This is the *athlete* who can tell you their VO max history in great detail... but can't remember the last time they went out on a Friday night to have a beer with their buddies.

# THE ONE-UPPER—"YOU RAN? I RAN MORE"

Ugh. The One-Upper. This is the worst kind of runner—and it isn't even close. There's something endearing or at least relatable about most of the profiles in this chapter. But this one? Nope. Nothing lovable here. Just pain.

This is the person who hijacks every running conversation. They don't ask questions—they just wait for you to take a breath so they can launch into their own story. Or opinion. Or both.

And the conversation doesn't even have to start out about running. No matter the topic, it'll be redirected toward their running achievements—whether you like it or not. (You don't.)

It doesn't matter what anyone in your group has accomplished—the One-Upper has done it better. And faster. Definitely faster. You finished a half-marathon in under two hours? Great. They did it in 1:30. With a broken leg. On a hilly course. Uphill both ways. In the snow. It never ends.

# THE BEER RUNNER—"FIRST THE MILES, THEN THE IPA"

If the One-Upper is the worst runner to hang out with, this next one might be the best. Sure, the Beer Runner has his faults—but you still want him at every post-run hangout. Why wouldn't you?

Judging by the evidence, this guy never actually trains. He signs up for races, sure. But there's no sign that he's done a single training run. He'll meet you for a pint after *your* workout, no problem. But did he run himself? Debatable.

And yet... somehow... he beats you. He shows up hungover on race morning, having stayed out late the night before, and still cranks out a decent time. As you fade in the final mile, he flies past you with a cheeky grin and a final surge. How the hell does he do it?

# THE COACH WHO COACHES NO ONE—"FORM CHECK? LET ME FILM YOU"

Ever get running advice from someone you definitely didn't ask? That's the Coach Who Coaches No One.

This guy is convinced he knows everything there is to know about running. Is he fast? Not really. But that doesn't stop him from doling out advice like he's been coaching Olympians for decades.

Where did he learn it all? YouTube, of course. He's spent hours absorbing wisdom about foot strike, cadence, vertical oscillation, and God knows what else. He talks like he has a PhD... but we're pretty sure he barely scraped through high school.

Should you listen to the unsolicited coaching? Probably not. Then again, he *did* watch a lot of videos, and you *might* be landing too far back on your heels... so... Nah. Ignore him.

# SOUND FAMILIAR?

You might have laughed. You might have cringed. You might have quietly realized that you've been a few of these runners — or worse, you still are. That's okay. We all are. Whether you're chasing segments, sprinting for the beer tent, or offering unsolicited advice at the start line, welcome to the tribe. This cast of characters is what makes running so gloriously weird, painfully honest, and weirdly addictive. Just try not to be too much of a One-Upper, yeah?

PHASE 2

# THE OBSESSOR
# (TRAINS HARD, TAPERS POORLY,
# LIES CONSTANTLY)

# RUNNING APPS, STATS, AND OTHER USELESS DATA

**4**

With the possible exception of breathing, nothing could be more natural than running. Humans have been doing it for as long as we've existed. For millennia, running was simply part of staying alive — catching food, avoiding predators, surviving another day.

And yet somehow, modern runners have turned this instinctual act into a full-blown nerd-fest. It's all about data now. Every run is another opportunity to harvest numbers that (supposedly) unlock the secrets of performance.

This approach to running might make sense if you are trying to qualify for the Olympics. Any little edge could mean the difference between taking home a medal or leaving empty-handed. It's harder to understand, however, for the runner who's trying to crack a 10-minute mile. Wouldn't it be more fun to just lace up the shoes and head out the door?

Apparently not. Runners as a whole have gone so deep into the data rabbit hole that there's no turning back at this point.

# FROM SURVIVAL TO SEGMENTS —
# THE FALL OF RUNNING'S SIMPLICITY

If you zoom out on the human timescale to look at where we started and where we are today, it's hard to believe we are the same species. The humans who once ran because they literally had to — their lives depended on it — are now running to jump to the top of a Strava segment in their neighborhood.

In some ways, running hasn't changed. It was hard then, and it's still hard now (though our ancestors probably weren't trying to get through a run after too many beers the night before). The motion is basically the same as it's always been — no matter what the latest online guru says about fixing your stride.

Imagine a group of early humans out on the plains thousands of years ago. They are waiting under the shade of a tree for the right time to head out on a hunt. When prey is in sight, they all run together, intense and powerful, until they get close enough to strike. It's an impressive performance and one that allows them to keep their families alive for at least a few more days. This was nature at its purest, and the stakes couldn't have been higher.

Fast-forward to today. A guy walks out of his two-story, air-conditioned home for a quick run before lunch.

He's wearing $2,000 worth of gear, and still complains that it's a bit warm for optimal performance. Instead of scanning the horizon for danger, he stares at his wrist, waiting for his GPS watch to link with satellites orbiting hundreds of miles above.

After laboring through two sluggish miles, he stumbles back inside, uploads his data to Strava, and limps into a hot shower. This modern man will now brag about his brave two-mile run for the next week, completely oblivious to the athletic achievements of his ancestors.

## THE GPS WATCH IS YOUR GOD NOW

It used to be that there were just two pieces of information available to runners about their performance: time and distance. That was it. You knew how far you ran, and you knew for how long. And, if you were capable with a bit of math, you could divide those two numbers and get a pace per mile or kilometer.

That was it. And it was more than enough. How did you know if you were getting better at running? Simple — you tracked your times for various distances to see if they were going down. Ran a 25-minute 5K last month and got it down to 24 minutes this month? Great! You've made progress and all is well.

Those simple, naïve days are long gone thanks to one particularly devious piece of technology — the GPS watch. Now that you can strap a monitor to your wrist and track everything you do on each run, the data has gotten out of control. Time and distance are still tracked, of course, but they're more of a starting point than a finish line.

You're already familiar with the ridiculous, obsessive patterns that a GPS watch can create. It causes you to check how much elevation you've gained when running down a perfectly flat road. It sends you into a panic when it mysteriously doesn't track your run or won't sync with your phone afterward.

Now that nearly everyone has a GPS watch of some kind, companies are having to find new ways to sell a fresh batch of these devices just to keep the profits flowing. It seems their strategy is to invent new metrics that are completely meaningless. Vertical oscillation? What the hell does that mean? And how could it possibly have anything to do with how fast you run a mile?

Speaking of things you don't really understand but pay attention to anyway — our next section covers that very topic.

# HEART RATE ZONES & TRAINING 'SCIENCE' YOU PRETEND TO UNDERSTAND

On a fundamental level, the human heart really only has two states — "on" and "off." For most of us, the goal of each day is simply to avoid winding up in the "off" category. As long as the heart is beating, it's been a good day.

Leave it to runners to make things more complicated. Now, there are Heart Rate Zones, and you have to be in the right one at all times or you might as well be dead. Specifically, you need to be in Zone 2. Are you in Zone 2? Why not? What's even the point of running if you aren't in Zone 2? Are you an idiot?!?!

To hear runners tell it, staying in Zone 2 throughout an entire run is the height of human existence. People who can run in Zone 2 are simply better than the rest of us — and that's just how it is. They're unlocking not only improved running times and an elevated level of fitness, but most likely, eternal life as well.

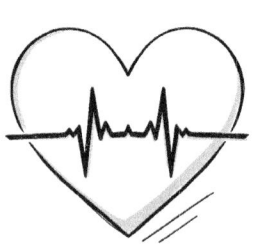

Heart Rate Zones range from 1 to 5. If you're in Zone 1, you should be ashamed — you lose the right to call yourself a runner. In Zone 2, as mentioned, you are a god. Zones 3 and 4 are reserved for intense tempo runs... or for morons who don't understand pacing.

And then there's Zone 5. This is the rarified air at the very edge of human physical capacity. It's only ever reached by those experiencing an impending bathroom emergency, with too far to go and not nearly enough time to get there.

## STRAVA: THE SOCIAL NETWORK THAT OWNS YOUR SOUL

We can all agree that social media is the downfall of modern society. Right? Great. Moving on.

With that groundwork in place, we can at least acknowledge that Strava is built around movement. It's not idle TikTok nonsense where you scroll through one pointless video after another until your eyes roll back into your head. Strava is about getting active, heading outside, and theoretically improving your health. On those grounds, it has our support.

So... how does it all go so wrong? It comes down to humans being humans. We can't just leave well enough alone. Instead of posting workouts and genuinely supporting each other, we turn it into a competitive mess. Segments to win. Weekly mileage to flex. Heart rate graphs to share. It quickly goes from a healthy habit to yet another source of stress and anxiety.

One of the most absurdly stressful parts of Strava life? Creating titles for your runs. There's an art to it. And the key rule: never admit to feeling good. You must always include something like *"legs felt heavy"* or *"shaking off some soreness."*

Downplaying how you felt makes the effort seem all the more heroic. No one is actually impressed, of course, but you'll feel a warm blanket of accomplishment when you hit "post" and assume your followers are in awe of your resilience.

## YOU'RE NOT TRAINING, YOU'RE COLLECTING NUMBERS

At this point, it's no longer running — it's math. And while there's nothing wrong with math, that's not exactly what you signed up for. You probably just wanted to get in shape, spend some time outside, and maybe meet a few like-minded people in your area.

Somehow, that pure and noble goal has devolved into late nights staring at spreadsheets, desperately hoping you'll uncover some magical insight that lets you reclaim that Strava segment currently owned by some jerk down the street.

Because let's be honest — at the end of the day, petty revenge is what running is really all about.

# INJURIES—
# BADGES OF HONOR

## 5

Runners get hurt. A lot. We're tempted to call this the "dirty secret" of running — only it's not a secret at all. Everyone knows runners are frequently injured, yet millions keep heading back out there day after day. It's hard to think of another activity that enjoys such regular participation despite the destruction it causes. Well... other than drinking, of course.

## IT STARTS SMALL (USUALLY)

If there's any good news about running injuries — and there isn't much — it's that most runners start off with relatively minor issues. Shin splints. Blisters. Muscle strains. The usual suspects. Uncomfortable, sure, but nothing serious.

These injuries are the gateway drug of the running world. You learn to brush them off. You certainly aren't going to let a blister stop you from logging miles. What you don't notice, though, is that these little aches are building up your pain tolerance in a dangerous way.

Running through shin splints? Normal. Blisters? No problem. But once you're okay being uncomfortable, it sets a precedent that can — and usually will — spiral out of control.

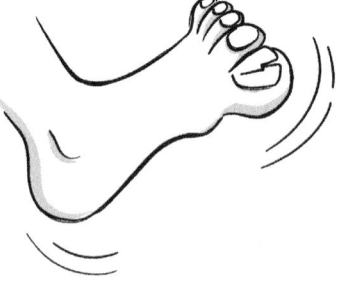

# DEEP IN DENIAL: TRAINING THROUGH PAIN

At some point, you'll go from toughing it out with a few minor issues to running while *legitimately* injured. Not sore. Not tired. Not a little stiff. **Injured.** But instead of seeing a doctor — or at least taking a few days off — you're still out there, slogging through mile after mile.

Is that kind of toughness admirable? Sure, to a degree. Is it smart? Most definitely not. You're almost certainly doing more harm than good, and sooner or later, you'll push it too far. That injury you've been ignoring? It's coming for you.

Enter: the dreaded plantar fasciitis — a rite of passage among runners. Mysterious. Frustrating. Painful. A stabbing sensation along the bottom of your foot with no clear cure. Just rest. And more rest. And then maybe some more rest after that.

At least it only bothers you while you're running, right? Ha — far from it. This painful condition will pester you at all times of the day and night. Those first steps you take out of bed in the morning when your alarm goes off? The stuff of nightmares.

Plantar fasciitis is just one example of how running injuries can wreck your daily life. A torn calf or strained quad might leave you limping for days. You might miss work. Skip family plans. Turn down invitations to things you'd normally enjoy. But hey — at least you're still holding onto that Strava segment. So it's all worth it... right?

## DIAGNOSED BY DR. GOOGLE

It's bad enough that runners continually hurt themselves by trying to keep running as the injuries pile up. What's even worse is the fact that plenty of runners don't even turn to a real doctor once it's clear that they're injured. After all, what's the point of making an appointment when Dr. Google is just a few clicks away?

Runners "know" more about the human body than anyone — except actual doctors. They're absolutely certain they've nailed the diagnosis based on five minutes of web searching. One solid Reddit thread featuring a bunch of equally clueless runners? That's all it takes to confirm their confident self-diagnosis.

These assumptions do more damage than good. What could have been solved quickly by an actual doctor with actual treatments now lingers for weeks, months... maybe years.

But who needs medical school, right? So what if doctors have decades of training and experience? Totally unnecessary. Apparently, all you need to diagnose and treat your running injuries is an internet connection and an inflated sense of certainty.

# PUTTING YOUR (PHYSIO'S) KIDS THROUGH COLLEGE

If you got into running to make friends, there's some good news: you're guaranteed to become close with one person in particular — your physio. You'll love them for the treatment. They'll love you for the steady stream of income that will fund several very nice family vacations.

Once you realize Dr. Google has been steering you wildly off-course, you start funneling most of your disposable income into physical therapy. The injuries keep piling up — or just won't go away — and eventually, you accept it's time to seek professional help. That's a smart move, but an expensive one.

With each visit, you get a little better... and a lot poorer. Every now and then, you question whether all this pain (and cost) is worth it. But those doubts don't last long. Surely the right combination of training tweaks and physio sessions will finally keep you healthy — next time.

And this time, you're committed. You do the exercises religiously. Every day. Sometimes twice a day. You even set calendar reminders. You excuse yourself from meetings to do your calf raises in the kitchen. You tell people it's part of your "injury prevention protocol" — which, technically, it is.

Until the moment you feel better.

Then? You start running again. The band gathers dust. The

exercises are forgotten. And within weeks, you're back at the physio's office getting the same routine, paying the same bill, and making the same promise: "I'll stick with the exercises this time." Sure you will.

But who has time for rehab when there are segments to steal and marathons to half-train for?

As you grow closer to your physio, he or she may even bring up the idea of dropping running in favor of a less punishing hobby. Insulted and offended, you storm out of the office and vow to find a doctor who understands your needs as an athlete.

**Note to Any Running Physios Reading This:** If you're a physio and you join a running club, you have two options: keep quiet or speak up. You might think speaking up is the smart

move — maybe you'll pick up a few clients. What actually happens? Free advice. Forever.

"Hey, quick one — got this weird tightness in my calf..."

You're not a club member anymore. You're now the unpaid on-call consultant. Good luck with that.

# WORSHIPPING AT THE ALTAR OF THE FOAM ROLLER

To hear a runner tell it, all you need to do to ward off injuries as the miles pile up is put in your time with the foam roller. This device, apparently, is a runner's best friend. It keeps you healthy, keeps your muscles loose, and ensures you're primed for the next big effort.

Or at least, that's the promise. Does it actually work that way? Eh, probably not. After all, if so many runners are religiously devoted to foam rolling, why are so many runners still injured? Hmmm. You'd think the effectiveness of this magical tube would have revealed itself by now.

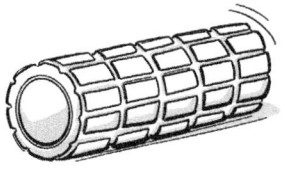

Maybe it doesn't do much good — but there is one thing a foam roller definitely delivers: pain. That's right. Under the guise of making you feel better, foam rolling will leave you gritting your teeth and sweating in agony. And weirdly, that's exactly what runners seem to love about it. They treat it like a badge of honor. They'll squirm and squeal through a session, then brag about it afterward like they've done something heroic.

Runners are a strange breed, indeed.

If you keep running, you're going to get hurt. Full stop. Does that mean you should quit? Not necessarily — that choice is yours. In the end, you might decide that the adoration of a few people at your local running club when you stagger across the 5k finish line in under 20 minutes is totally worth cutting decades off the useful life of your knees.

It's your call.

# RACE DAY MADNESS

## 6

For a runner, few things are as exciting as race day. Depending on the length of the race, you might have been training for this occasion for weeks, months, or even years. A ton of blood, sweat, and tears goes into race prep, and you want everything to go perfectly.

Of course, it won't. Not even close. Most race day experiences are a slow-motion circus of tiny disasters — runners obsessing over every detail until the gun finally goes off and launches them into full-blown chaos. By the end, you swear you'll never do this again... until the next sign-up form appears and so does your credit card.

This chapter is here to help you make sense of the madness. Whether you've run a dozen marathons or just finished your first 5k, what follows might hit a little too close to home.

## THE NIGHT BEFORE

Getting a great night of sleep before a big race is critical. It's also impossible.

Trying to sleep the night before a race is like trying to sleep before surgery (which, if you keep running, might not be a hypothetical). You

know you need to rest to give yourself the best shot at success, but your brain has other plans.

Two things will happen — either you'll finally drift off about an hour before your alarm goes off, or you'll be so wired that you're up hours before it ever rings.

So, you toss and turn. All. Night. Long.

You stare across the room at the outfit you've already laid out on the floor — carefully arranged, photographed, and posted for a humble-brag on Instagram.

And while you are awake, you keep checking the weather. Again. And again. As if anything is going to change. The weather forecasters have long since called it a day, but here you are, refreshing anyway.

## THE WAKE-UP CALL

Eventually, your alarm goes off at some ungodly hour. Not that you needed it — you were already awake. Feeling anything but refreshed, you shuffle into the shower, and that's when the nerves really hit. This is it. Just a shower and a short drive now separate you from the start line.

It all seemed like a great idea six months ago when you signed up with a friend. But now? You actually have to *run* this thing? What a colossal mistake.

For weeks, you've been planning what to eat on race morning. Fueling is critical, after all. But now you're second-guessing everything. Should you really eat that banana? It looks a bit off. And that bagel? It has mid-race diarrhea written all over it. Everything feels like a trap. One wrong decision — no matter how small — could derail the entire race.

Despite the neurotic behavior that you can't escape, the minutes keep ticking by, and soon enough, it's time to leave. With your heart in your throat like you're headed out for a first date — or your own execution — you do your best to act cool. Like you're not completely sh***ing it.

## NAVIGATING THE PORTA-POTTY GAUNTLET

Have you ever wondered how porta-potty companies stay in business? It's running races. That's it. Book a few events a year and your chemical toilet empire is secured.

Joking aside, the demand for porta-potties at the start of a race is insane. Everyone's been hydrating obsessively for the last 24 hours, and there's only one inevitable outcome. That fluid has

to go somewhere — and that somewhere is into a cramped plastic box that somehow smells like feet, antiseptic, and death. A dignified experience this is not.

The moment you arrive at the race, you've got two priorities: check in, and get in line. The porta-potty queue is its own endurance challenge — shuffling nervously, avoiding eye contact, trying to calculate who looks like they're about to explode. You *think* you can wait until Mile 4. You cannot.

Because if the hydration doesn't get you, the nerves almost certainly will. You might be a once-a-day, regular-as-clockwork kind of person. But on race day? All bets are off. The combination of anxiety, adrenaline, and that slightly suspect banana you forced down earlier is about to turn you into a human espresso machine.

Let's not sugarcoat it: you're going to need a number two. And you're going to need it *fast*.

Suddenly, it's a desperate game of porta-potty roulette. You scan the row of plastic thrones, trying to guess which one has the shortest wait — and the least psychological damage inside. Every second you hesitate, another runner snatches your spot, and your odds of getting stuck behind someone settling in for their own "situation" go up exponentially.

There are no friends in this line. No small talk. No mercy. Just tense, sweaty stares into the middle distance as everyone prays for their turn. It's every runner for themselves.

Because missing the start gun is unfortunate.

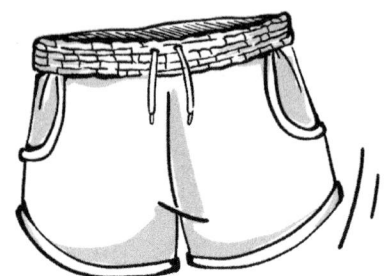

Missing the toilet? That's a full-blown race day catastrophe.

## FACING THE START LINE

The moment is finally here. You've been to the bathroom (twice). You've adjusted your bib five times to make sure it looks perfect in your post-race pictures. There's nothing left to do but wait for the starting gun and head out into this intimidating journey.

In the packed huddle of humanity at the start line, a few things become clear. First, some of these people definitely lied about their estimated pace. That guy claims he's aiming for a sub-three-hour marathon? Please. He looks like the only time he's run recently was to catch the buffet before it closed.

You'll also realize that running brings out some truly strange characters. Why is that woman blasting music out of a speaker when the rest of us live in the age of headphones? And what's with the people doing jumping jacks or sprinting back and forth before the race even begins? Are they planning to burn all their energy *before* the gun goes off?

For as much as you've been fearing the race, now you can't wait for it to start. Anything to get away from these people.

## SETTLING IN — FOR A WHILE

If you're running a relatively long race — anything half marathon or longer — there's usually a brief, magical moment when things start to click. The crowd thins out, the adrenaline dips just enough, and you find a rhythm. The chaos of the start is behind you. You're cruising now. It feels almost... peaceful. Like a nice training run. In the best way possible.

This blissful state will last approximately half a mile.

That "zone" you found? Gone. The flow turns to flailing. Your lungs are on fire because — let's be honest — you went out way too fast. Everyone goes out too fast. It's race day law. And now the lactic acid is knocking on the door like it's got a delivery you didn't order.

That hot spot in your shoe? It's growing. Thanks, stranger who stomped on your foot at the start. And those people you flew past in Mile 1? They're starting to reel you in, one smug step at a time.

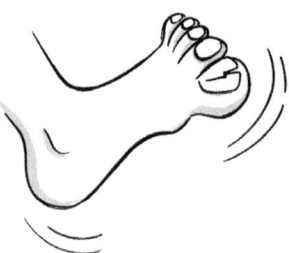

By the halfway point, you're bargaining with the universe. Never again, you promise. Never again will you subject yourself to this ridiculous punishment. This is your last race, forever. No question. Zero doubt.

(We'll revisit that feeling in a moment.)

## ENCOUNTERING THE COSTUME RUNNERS

As the race wears on, your attention shifts back to the people around you. It was best to block them out for a while after the circus that was the starting line, but now they're serving a new purpose: distraction. If you can look at — and silently judge — other runners, it'll help take your mind off your own suffering and steadily fading split times.

That's when something becomes glaringly obvious. Some of these people — far too many of them, in fact — are wearing costumes. But why? Were they dressed like this at the starting line, or did they pull off a mid-race outfit change? You must have been too focused on your bladder to notice the parade of ridiculous getups surrounding you.

Part of you wants to embrace the silliness and accept the costumes as part of the race day fun. It's kind of charming, after all. But you can't quite get there. It feels like an insult to the sport. Worse — it feels personal.

You've been training like an Olympian for six months, investing in the latest gear to reduce drag, wick away moisture, and squeeze out every possible second. And yet, here you are, getting absolutely destroyed in the final miles by a guy dressed as a giant banana.

What the hell.

# WATER STATIONS & FUELLING—
# THE MID-RACE GAMBLE

The one golden rule of race day? Never try anything new. Why? Because your body and mind are already operating in a state of mild (okay, severe) panic. Introducing an unfamiliar element — be it gear, pacing, or fuel — is a fast-track ticket to disaster.

But of course, that rule gets thrown out the window the moment you see a table lined with brightly colored cups and shiny foil gel packets. You've trained for months. You're prepared. You told yourself you wouldn't touch anything you hadn't practiced with. And yet... twenty minutes in, there you are — grabbing at gels like a kid in a candy store.

Let's break it down:

- **Water:** Great in theory. In practice? Try drinking out of a half-crushed paper cup while running. Half goes up your nose, the other half down your shirt. But hey — you're hydrated now. Kind of.

- **Energy Drink**: You didn't train with it. You promised yourself you'd avoid it. "It's only a 5k," you said. But now your lips are suspiciously sticky and your mouth tastes like radioactive citrus. It begins.

- **Gels**: The big one. You know you shouldn't. But you do. They're sweet. They're weirdly warm. And they promise energy, so you take two. Maybe three. You get a hit of sugar, maybe even a runner's high... followed immediately by the threat of a gastrointestinal meltdown.

If you're lucky, it's just a wave of regret. If you're not, you'll be bent over with stomach cramps or queuing up mid-race for the on-course porta-potty, sweating, pacing, and praying it's not occupied. And if it is? You're running your fastest splits of the day looking for the next one.

Race day fuelling: a high-risk, high-sugar gamble. Play carefully.

# CROSSING THE LINE

Against all odds, the finish line comes into view. Wait—have you done it? You've done it! You're actually going to finish the race... and you're not even in last place! It feels like a tremendous accomplishment, and before you've even caught your breath, you're already checking the date for next year's race so you can save it to your calendar.

Remember how you swore off running forever back at Mile 9? That was just a moment. You and running were having one of your little fights. You always do this—dramatic declarations mid-race, only to make up afterwards. It's a complicated relationship, but as long as you get across the line in one piece, you'll always be back.

Races aren't the only reason to become a runner—but they do lock in your status. Once you've experienced the highs and lows (mostly lows) of dragging yourself through a finish line, it's like a drug. You want another hit. Because the next one? That's the one that'll go smoothly. That's the one you'll get right.

Right?

Because now you want to go further. Faster. Sub-3:30 marathon? Sure—why not?

Because once you're a runner, there's always something next. Always another milestone to chase, another distance to tick off, another PR to beat. Even if you say you don't care, the game of one-upmanship never really ends.

Especially with yourself.

## BASKING IN THE GLORY (A WEEK LATER)

You've done it. You crossed the line, you didn't die, and now you're floating somewhere between exhaustion and euphoria. You feel like an absolute legend — and, for a brief, glorious window, you are. For 24 hours, you're basically a minor celebrity.

People want to hear your story. "How far was it again?" they ask, genuinely impressed — or at least pretending well. You recount the highs, the lows, the hot spots on your feet, the emotional rollercoaster of Mile 9, and the heroic surge at the end (which, in reality, was more of a wobbly shuffle — but that's not the point).

And then there's the medal.

Oh, the medal. That glorious hunk of metal, ribbon, and validation. It might weigh less than your phone, but emotionally, it's heavier than gold. You earned this. It says, "I did it." It says, "I am capable of greatness." It says, "Please notice me, I ran a race."

## So now the question: how long can you reasonably wear it?

To the finish line festival? Absolutely. That medal is your entry pass to smug satisfaction and perhaps a free banana.

To the pub afterwards? Definitely. In fact, it may earn you a round or two from strangers, or at the very least, a nod of respect from fellow medal-clad warriors. It's like being in an exclusive, sweaty, limping club.

The next day? Well... that's where things get tricky.

Wearing it to work? Bold move. Admirable in its audacity. Sure, you might claim it was "accidental" and that you "forgot" it was still on — but everyone knows you practiced your dramatic "Oh this old thing?" line in the mirror that morning. It's fine. We get it. You ran a race. Just... maybe take it off before the 3 p.m. meeting.

Eventually, though, the medal finds its place. It hangs proudly in your hallway, office, or (let's be honest) Instagram bio. A gleaming reminder that once, you were a badass. Once, you conquered pain, doubt, and bowel uncertainty — and came out victorious.

And if that doesn't earn a permanent spot on the wall, what does?

# THE PHILOSOPHER (DELUSIONAL BUT PEACEFUL ABOUT IT)

# THE BULLSH*T RUNNERS SAY (AND WHAT IT REALLY MEANS)

## 7

You know how fishermen have a reputation for lying about pretty much everything? You can put runners in the same category. There's something about being out there alone for all those hours, racking up mile after mile, that causes you to say some wild (and completely made-up) things.

If you're new to running, it might be a little jarring at first to hear how runners talk. All these stories can't be true, right? Do these people actually know what they're saying? In time, you'll learn it's mostly nonsense — but it takes a while to spot the bullsh*t.

If you find yourself struggling to decode what your new runner friends are talking about, we'll clear it up below.

## CASUAL LIES

In general, the lies runners tell are harmless. In fact, they aren't even serious all the time. They are somewhat tongue-in-cheek. These are the casual lies that we all spew but they don't really bother anyone or cause any problems.

So, why do we keep lying if the lies don't really matter? Who knows. It's just part of the game. You've probably heard (or said) some of these yourself:

- **"I'm just running this 5k for fun."** I'll be killing myself down the home stretch to chase a PR.

- **"I don't look at my watch much when I run."** I check it every minute for pace and cadence stats.

- **"It's not about time — I'm just here for the experience."** I obsess over my times and hate losing.

- **"I haven't really been training for this race."** All I do is train — it's ruining my work/life balance.

- **"I ran a few miles yesterday but feel great today."** My legs are jelly and I'm going to fall over.

- **"I could've gone faster if I wanted to."** That was everything I had. I'm just really slow.

- **"That hill wasn't too bad."** I thought I was going to die halfway up.

- **"Let's take it easy today."** I'll lull you into relaxing, then drop the hammer at the end.

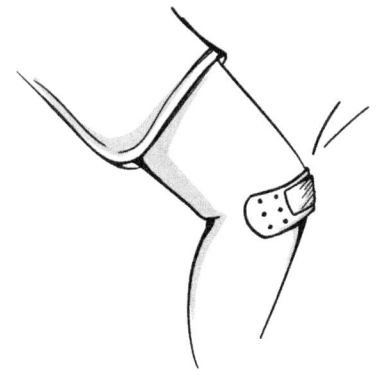

# TRAINING TALL TALES

The beauty of training is that it usually happens alone. And that means — — yep — we can lie. And we do. Unless you post your workout data to Strava like an amateur, you're free to make up whatever you want when swapping stories with others. Even if you *do* post it, there's always the classic fallback: "My watch glitched — it didn't log the last five miles."

Runners love stretching the truth about training because it makes us look like the real deal. Anyone can clock a decent time on race day with the crowd cheering and adrenaline pumping. But holding pace for hours in a solo training run with no witnesses? That's elite-level stuff. Or at least, that's the myth we like people to buy.

- **"I only did 12 miles this morning."** Including the three miles that I drove to the trailhead and the three miles I drove home.

- **"My coach says I need to slow down my training pace — I'm going out too fast."** I don't have a coach, and I've never run at a pace that could be described as "too fast".

- **"I ran a negative split in my workout today."** I don't know what that means, but I heard somebody say it on YouTube.

- **"Didn't even break a sweat on that five-miler."** I sweat so much that I'm throwing these shorts away.

- **"I ran an out and back and there was a headwind both ways."** There wasn't a single breath of wind, but I needed an excuse.

- **"I never skip leg day."** And by "leg day" I mean walking to the fridge.

- **"I was listening to my body today."** My body told me to stop at McDonald's halfway through.

- **"Just a recovery run."** I pushed hard the whole way but labelled it 'easy' on Strava.

# PRE-RACE AND RACE-DAY NONSENSE

Nowhere in the running world is there more bluster than the pre-race corral. Everyone's wired, competitive, and ready to start broadcasting their greatness to anyone within earshot.

And it doesn't stop once the gun goes off. Some runners will keep up the chatter mid-race, and most will definitely resume the performance once they cross the finish line. Sound familiar?

- **"I don't even get nervous for races anymore."** I'm so nervous, I haven't slept in three days.

- **"This is just another long run. I do workouts harder than this all the time."** I haven't run this far in months — and I never finish my long runs anyway.

- **"I've spent the last two weeks tapering for this race."** I'm injured and in denial, so I stopped running and decided to call it tapering.

- **"I don't really care where I place in this race. I'm just enjoying the experience."** I've checked the age group rankings three times already.

- **"I felt great the whole time out there."** I was cursing at strangers by Mile 7 and swore I'd never run again.

- **"I hope you have a great race — I'd love to see you get a PR."** I'm secretly rooting against you. I'll trip you if I have to.

- **"I think this course was longer than it should've been."** I'm out of shape but prefer to blame the course.

# BRAGGING IN DISGUISE

Runners have mastered the art of the humble brag. It's a thing of beauty, and no group of people does it better. They know the things they are doing are impressive in the sense that they are out of reach for the average person, yet they have to frame these accomplishments like they are no big deal. It would be tremendously annoying if it wasn't such a well-crafted art form.

These disguised brags come in many flavors. You've probably heard a few. You've probably *said* a few.

- **"It was just a light run."** That was the hardest I've pushed myself in weeks.

- **"I must've burned 1,000 calories on my run this morning."** And then I ate 2,000 immediately after and called it "recovery."

- **"I'm on a recovery week, so I'm only doing 35 miles."** I haven't seen my kids in months.

- **"My legs feel great after my run today."** I mean, I can't feel them at all, which is actually kind of nice.

- **"I don't find running painful — it's a beautiful struggle."** I've been swearing under my breath since mile two.

- **"I ran a slower pace today just to keep things easy — only 8 minutes per mile."** That's the fastest I've *ever* run, and I need you to be impressed.

- **"I didn't realize until after that I had a couple of blisters on my toes."** All my toenails are dead. But I'm pretending I don't care.

- **"I only upload hard runs to Strava — I don't need attention for everything."** I live on Strava. I refresh my follower count like it's the stock market.

The funny thing about the way runners lie is that, at first, you'll be convinced that you are never going to be one of them. You are above that kind of childish behavior, after all.

Then one day, after a 60-mile training week, you catch yourself spinning tales that no reasonable person would believe.

And just like that — you've joined the club.

RUN PRO

# YOU KNOW YOU'RE
# A RUNNER WHEN...

## 8

## Running Hall of Fame

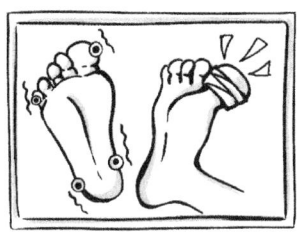
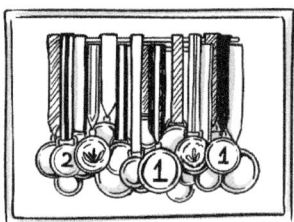

Are you a runner? Simple question, tricky answer.

Some people run regularly but don't consider themselves "real runners." They just head out for a jog a few times a week and think nothing of it. Others run once a week — *maybe* — yet won't shut up about how much of a runner they are.

So who knows? What counts as a runner to one person might not even register to another. And in the end, the definition probably doesn't matter.

Still, if you're wondering whether you've fully crossed the line into full-blown "runner" status, this chapter will help. There are certain things you say, do, or own that make your status pretty clear. We've broken it into categories to make it easier to digest.

Let's start with the obvious one.

## GEAR OBSESSIONS

We've already spent a lot of time in this book discussing runners and their gear. And for good reason. Countless dollars are poured into the pursuit of faster times and more enjoyable runs — despite the fact that running is always going to be miserable at some point, no matter what you're wearing. But that doesn't stop us.

Runners will continue chasing that magical pair of shoes, the miracle shorts, the perfect watch setting... something to finally make this masochistic hobby feel fun. (It's too late to take up golf anyway.)

So, if any of the following feel a little too familiar, congratulations: you're not just a runner—you're a *gear-obsessed* runner.

You know you're that kind of runner when...

- You own more running shoes than all other shoes combined.

- You wear compression socks—even when you're not running.

- Not only do you use anti-chafe balm, but you've tested them all and ranked your favorites.

- 90% of your laundry is moisture-wicking.

- You know more about GPS watch battery life than a Garmin sales rep.

- You keep reordering the same shorts in bulk for fear they'll be discontinued.

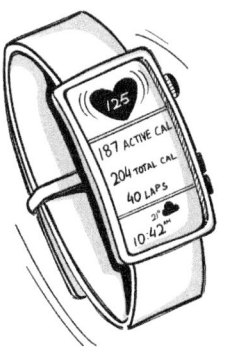

- You wear running sunglasses at night "just in case."

- You have strong, emotional opinions about sock thickness and blister prevention.

- Your garage features at least five foam rollers in different sizes and textures.

- You display your GPS watch collection like some people display Rolexes.

More signs to come... but if you've nodded along to most of these, yeah — you're in.

## STRANGE HABITS

Runners do some strange sh*t. But you don't need us to tell you that.

Any time someone spends hours alone in a difficult, demanding pursuit, they're bound to pick up some weird habits along the way.

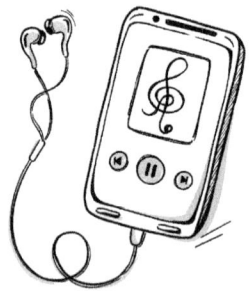

To outsiders, these look like quirks. Or full-blown disorders. But to runners? Perfectly normal. Expected, even.

So if the list below seems totally reasonable to you — you're already in the club.

You know you've developed some strange running habits when...

- You run laps in your driveway after a run just to get your total distance up to the next round mile.

- You check the weather forecast five times a day to time your run just right.

- You regularly leave social events early on a Saturday night because you have to do your long run on Sunday morning.

- Eating dinner at 4:30 p.m. so you can get to bed early seems completely normal.

- You know where every public toilet is on your route — and have them ranked by cleanliness.

- You casually drop "tempo pace" into conversations that have nothing to do with running.

- You can't remember your kids' birthdays, but you know your PRs for five distances.

- You've taped your nipples to prevent chafing — even though you're not running today.

- Your phone is full of Garmin screenshots and almost zero pictures of your family.

- You haven't planned a vacation in years that wasn't built around a running race.

# SOCIAL CLUES

Interactions between runners and normal people are always a bit awkward. And no — before you ask — runners don't count as normal people. You already knew that, but it's best just to acknowledge it and move on.

Non-runners can't imagine being interested in the things you obsess over. Negative splits. The glycemic load of gels and chews. How to give yourself a proper pedicure to avoid discovering a bloody sock after a 12-mile run. You know — the usual.

These social signs are less about the act of running and more about the things you do or say that make other people shake their heads... or slowly back away.

You know you are a runner with unusual social patterns when...

- The only selfies on your Instagram are post-run and dripping with sweat.

- You discuss your foot blisters over lunch — at work.

- All your friends have muted your notifications because they know it's just more running stuff.

- The only new friends you ever make are people you recognize from the trails.

- You regularly turn down social plans because "you've got a race that weekend."

- Before showering — or even peeing — you check Strava.

- You don't follow any actors or musicians on Instagram, but you do follow at least a dozen pro runners.

- There's always a pair of running shoes in your car — because "you never know."

- You consider a moisture-wicking tee and three-inch shorts totally acceptable party wear.

- You skip your nephew's birthday party because it doesn't fit your training cycle.

- You can identify acquaintances from across the park... just by their gait.

## PHYSICAL EVIDENCE

You might be able to deny many of the signs we've listed so far. It's not too hard to fool yourself into thinking that these things don't really describe you. Or maybe a few hit close to home — but not *all* of them, right?

But the physical evidence doesn't lie. And it's everywhere. Whether it's your body, your home, or the contents of your car, the reality of your runner lifestyle becomes clear when you start piecing together the clues — like a detective tracking down a suspect. Spoiler: the suspect is you.

The physical evidence points to you being a runner when...

- Your tan lines look like you've been wearing the same socks and shorts for a decade.

- Your medal rack needs reinforced screws to hold the weight.

- You have an entire drawer dedicated to old race bibs (and yes, you're keeping them all).

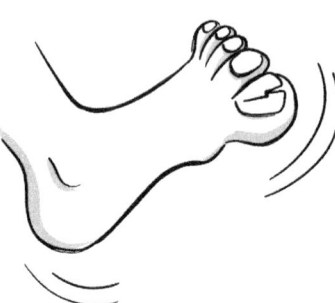

- Your feet look like you've run every race barefoot — and through a gravel pit.

- Your dreams are about running. So are your nightmares.

- Your knees and elbows are permanently scarred from "controlled falls" on the trail.

- You limp everywhere — except on race day, when you somehow run just fine.

- Your shorts are crusted with old gel residue that leaked months ago.

- Your face has taken on a rugged, leathery texture from years of sun exposure.

So... are you a runner?

You might still be on the fence — but after reading those lists, you probably have a better idea.

If none of these sound familiar, congratulations — you've managed to avoid full-blown runner status. For now. But don't get too comfortable. It's coming for you.

And if you *do* tick every box? Our condolences. You're in deep now. Being a runner is a life sentence. You might as well embrace it.

Now get back out there. Those miles aren't going to run themselves.

PHASE 4

# THE LIFER
# (NUMB LEGS, FULL HEART,
# CAN'T QUIT)

# THE BUCKET LIST (THAT YOU'LL NEVER FINISH) 9

Every runner eventually builds a bucket list of things they want to do before they (supposedly) hang up their running shoes. You probably don't start out that way — you just want to run — but over time, the list begins to form. A collection of goals, experiences, and delusions that feels both exciting and totally unrealistic.

The funny thing? Most runners' lists look exactly the same. Ask ten runners for their bucket list and you'll get near-identical responses. It's as if no one in this sport can think for themselves.

In this chapter, we're taking a look at the greatest hits — the running bucket list items that pop up again and again. Will you tick them all off? Probably not. But dreaming about them helps the miles go by a little faster.

## FINISH A MARATHON

This is the obvious place to start. It doesn't take long to go from, "Hey, I'm going to head out for a run," to, "Hey, I think I'm going to train for a marathon." There's something strangely magical about the completely arbitrary distance of 26.2 miles that grabs the imagination and refuses to let go.

Of course, we'd be lying if we said this bucket list item was all about personal growth and achievement. Those might be nice side effects — but the primary motivation? Ego. You want to call yourself a marathon runner. You want to look down on people who haven't.

"Oh, you did a local charity 5K? That's adorable. I do 5Ks for recovery. Good for you though."

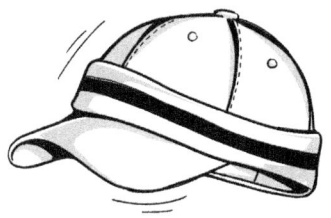

That said, finishing a marathon is probably within reach — if you apply yourself and don't mind taking forever to do it. As long as you can beat the sweeper at a few checkpoints along the way, you should be able to knock it out and wear that finisher's medal with pride for the rest of your life.

## A GEOGRAPHICAL CHECKLIST

Another classic entry on the runner's bucket list: some wildly ambitious goal involving running in as many different places as possible. The specifics vary from person to person, but these dreams are usually as unrealistic as they are oddly specific.

Maybe you want to run in all 50 U.S. states. Or hit every continent — excluding Antarctica... or including it, because why not freeze your face off for bragging rights? Maybe your thing is running trails in every National Park or sprinting to the top of iconic peaks.

It's easy to dream big when you've got Google Maps and a few hours to kill. It gets a bit harder when you have to get down to the matter of planning these adventures out in a practical sense. When exactly are you going to take the time off work? And more importantly — who's funding this international jog-fest?

This is one of those bucket list items that tends to go unfulfilled. Real life has a habit of getting in the way. Unless your geographical goal is something a little more doable — like running every 5K in your local county — you might need to make peace with the fact that this one's staying on the "dream" list.

## JOIN THE "STREAK" CLUB

No, joining the "streak" club in running doesn't mean ditching your shorts for the last few hundred meters of a marathon. Although, that's an idea worth exploring in its own right.

What we're talking about here is building a running streak: consecutive days where you lace up your shoes and hit the pavement. You set your own

rules, but most runners agree that a streak-worthy run needs to be at least one mile.

This one's just attainable enough to become a full-blown obsession. After all, it's only a mile — how hard can that be? Depending on your pace, you're done in 10 minutes. Do it again tomorrow. And the next day. And before you know it, you're deep into a streak you can't bear to break.

RUN PRO

In case you're wondering, the longest recorded running streak is over 50 years — so you'd better start today.

## RUN IN A RIDICULOUS COSTUME

Remember that chapter where we talked about getting smoked in a marathon by some idiot in a banana suit? That could be you! Well — maybe not the part where you breeze past other runners at an impressive pace dressed as tropical produce. But definitely the part about being the idiot in the costume.

And don't feel limited to bananas. The sky's the limit when it comes to ridiculous outfits that conveniently distract from the fact you're a mediocre runner at best. Want to be a hot dog for a 5K? Go for it. Superman for a 10K? Why not.

Or, better yet — combine your love of running with a creative costume choice and go for a title. Find something obscure enough, and you might just snag yourself a Guinness World Record as the "fastest half marathon dressed as a jellyfish." Yes, that's a thing. Probably.

Without a doubt, this is the easiest bucket list item to tick off. Order something ridiculous, sign up for a race, and prepare to be simultaneously cheered, laughed at, and maybe even immortalized in record books for the dumbest reason imaginable.

## QUALIFY FOR BOSTON

Now we're getting serious. As far as running goals go for the average runner, they don't get much loftier than qualifying for the Boston Marathon. This is the pinnacle of amateur competition — and hitting a Boston qualifying time is the stuff of dreams.

It's not going to happen, of course. The odds of surviving an entire training cycle uninjured *and* running the race of your life to hit a BQ time? Astronomical. But hey, it's a nice dream.

Luckily, there's a workaround. Boston holds a limited number of spots for charity runners. That's how you get in when you're slow. So... time to hit up your rich friends.

# FINISH A TRAIL RUN—
# WITHOUT GETTING LOST

Trail running is practically a different sport from road racing. Sure, both involve putting one foot in front of the other—but that's about where the similarities end. On the road, you can zone out, throw on some music or a podcast, and just cruise. There's something almost meditative about a long road run when you're in good enough shape to settle into the rhythm.

Trail running? Not so much. Instead, your eyes are locked on the ground, scanning every step for roots, rocks, and other ankle-destroying hazards. And if the terrain doesn't get you, the wildlife might. Every rustle in the bushes sends a jolt to your lizard brain. Bears? Coyotes? Angry squirrels? Who knows. What a lovely, relaxing way to spend your Saturday.

Still, this one sticks to your bucket list. You like the *idea* of running through a quiet forest, emerging from the trees at sunset looking like a triumphant hero. That is, unless you miss a turn, end up in a bog behind a pig farm, and realize—wait... that *is* mud, right?

# ENTER AN ULTRAMARATHON

The hubris required to enter an ultramarathon is just off the charts. A regular marathon? Pfft... too easy. Only 26.2 miles? What are we, in preschool? Talk to me when you have a real challenge lined up.

So, naturally, you decide to take it up a notch and sign up for an ultramarathon. These races vary in distance, but 50- and even 100-mile events are common. That's a number that's hard to even *comprehend* — until you're out there, somewhere in the middle of it, questioning every life choice that led to this moment.

Often, ultramarathons are held on trails, so you could technically knock out two bucket list items at once — if you manage to crawl across the finish line on your bloodied knees a few seconds before the time limit expires. At least your overpriced race vest will finally feel justified. Just don't forget to pack a charger for your GPS watch and phone. You're going to be out there for a *long* time.

# EXPERIENCE A DESTINATION RACE (RACECATION!)

This last bucket list item overlaps a bit with the geographical goals we talked about earlier — but it's a little different. Instead of simply wanting to run in different places, you're entering a *specific* race and turning it into a vacation. In other words, you're choosing to let a running event ruin what could have been a perfectly good holiday.

The options are endless. As long as you've got the money and some time off work, you can make it happen. Maybe you'll sign up for a half marathon at Disneyland. Maybe you'll choose a race in some dramatic, picturesque location so you can flood your Instagram with likes. Wherever you go, one thing's guaranteed: you'll injure yourself rushing through the airport and end up limping through the entire race — smiling through gritted teeth and pretending to enjoy every minute.

# GET OUT THERE AND ENJOY IT

We've spent this chapter (and most of this book) having fun at the expense of runners. But in all seriousness, there's nothing wrong with having a running bucket list. This is an aspirational hobby, and even if you fall short of ticking every box, at least you're out there moving, sweating, and occasionally suffering. That's got to count for something.

So go out there, explore, tick off those lists, see the world—and most importantly, stay fit and enjoy the ride!

# CONCLUSION

You've made it to the end of the book. Much like your last 10k, it was probably a struggle to cross the finish line, but here we are. Not necessarily triumphant, sure, but we made it nonetheless.

We hope you've recognized yourself in some of the characters, race-day rituals, and gear obsessions we've shared along the way. Oh, who are we kidding? Of course you have — they *are* you. With every stride, you take a step deeper into the inner circle of running madness.

At this point, you're no longer just a runner. You're a case study. A case study in obsessive, irrational behavior. But that's not necessarily as bad as it sounds. It might not make much sense to be so passionate about a hobby that has you running for hours only to end up right back where you started. But there are worse ways to spend your time.

## RUNNING IS THE BEST WORST HOBBY

All of the criticisms we have leveled at running throughout this book are true. We stand behind them completely.

At the same time, running is still a great hobby. It might be hard to believe that all of the nasty downsides to this sport can be offset by the positives, but that's just how it is. And that's why so many people keep on running, mile after mile, with no end in sight.

Sure, running is time-consuming. A long run can easily eat up most of your Sunday and leave you drained come Monday. And yes, running hurts. Even if you avoid injury — which you won't — you'll still be permanently sore, and people will look at you funny when you walk into the office.

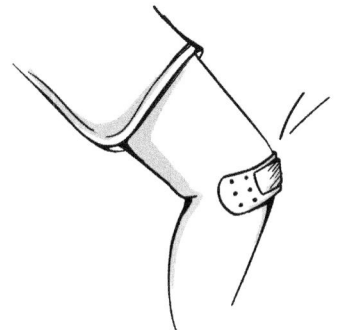

And don't even get us started on the cost. For a sport that *should* be affordable, it's ruinously expensive. The $300 shoes. The high-tech apparel. The gadgets. While you *should* be saving for retirement, you're instead "investing" in products that might shave a second or two off your PR.

But none of that matters. It really doesn't. This is a beautiful hobby full of wonderful people. Crazy people, yes — but wonderful people nonetheless. You love the sport, and it's way too late to turn back now. You're a runner. You might as well own it.

# YOU'LL NEVER QUITE BE SATISFIED

The best hobbies always have something just out of reach. They can't be mastered. No matter how fast you get, there will always be more seconds to shave off, technical tweaks to make, new distances or courses to conquer.

It might seem ironic in a sport defined by finish lines, but there's no end to the running journey. And that might just be the best part.

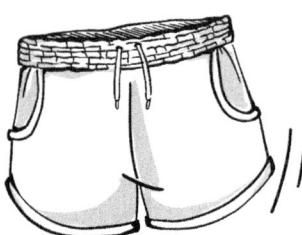

Running is a lot like golf this way. No one has ever played a perfect round — you can always improve. The same goes for running. You get to keep chasing the best version of yourself, on road or trail, for a lifetime. And probably will.

# A FEW MORE TIPS

We couldn't wrap up without leaving you with a few more — completely unhelpful — tips to take on your next run (or between runs). Let's have a little fun before we go:

- Start every run by questioning every life choice that led you here.

- If your leg hurts, ice it. If it still hurts, just keep running.

- Rest days are important — as long as your rest day still includes a 5K.

- No matter how fast you get, a tiny dog will always trot past you on the sidewalk.

- If you don't tell everyone you know you've entered a race, it doesn't count.

- Buy the shoes. You're going to anyway, so just get it over with.

- Don't take yourself too seriously. But still show up in lycra to win.

What do we want you to take away from this book? Above all else: strip away any pretense that you aren't head-over-heels obsessed with running. It's okay — we are too. The sport makes no sense. It's a terrible idea for a million reasons. And that stops no one.

Keep going. Keep chasing PRs you'll never break. Keep trying to outrun people half your age. As long as you're laughing along the way, it's all worth it.

Enjoy!

BEMBERTON
BOOKS

# LEAVE A REVIEW

If this book made you laugh—or at least feel slightly better about black toenails and foam rolling—drop a quick review or star rating on Amazon.

It helps other runners (and the people who put up with them) find the book—and know they're not alone in the madness of running.

## To leave a review & help spread the word

Printed in Dunstable, United Kingdom

75583768R00067